A COMPASSIONATE CALL TO COUNTER CULTURE
IN A WORLD OF UNREACHED PEOPLE GROUPS

A COMPASSIONATE CALL TO

COUNTER CULTURE

IN A WORLD OF
UNREACHED PEOPLE GROUPS

DAVID PLATT

TYNDALE HOUSE PUBLISHERS, INC., CAROL STREAM, ILLINOIS

Visit Tyndale online at www.tyndale.com.

TYNDALE and Tyndale's quill logo are registered trademarks of Tyndale House Publishers, Inc.

A Compassionate Call to Counter Culture in a World of Unreached People Groups

Copyright © 2015 by David Platt. All rights reserved.

Designed by Dean H. Renninger

Scripture quotations are taken from *The Holy Bible*, English Standard Version® (ESV®), copyright © 2001 by Crossway, a publishing ministry of Good News Publishers. Used by permission. All rights reserved.

ISBN 978-1-4964-0587-6 (sampler). Order full product under ISBN 978-1-4143-7329-4.

Printed in the United States of America

21	20	19	18	17	16	15
7	6	5	4	3	2	1

Dear Reader,

I am increasingly burdened by the current climate in our culture—and in the church—on prevailing social issues. Battles are raging today over issues such as sexuality, marriage, poverty, sex trafficking, abortion, orphan care, racism, immigration, and religious liberty. I believe we have a deep need to consider how Christ compels us to respond to each of these issues in the culture around us.

Our zeal for some social issues may be applauded, while our stand on other, more controversial issues will bring criticism. Either way, we must not be content to sit down and stay quiet. Our goal is neither comfort in nor approval from the surrounding culture. We must stand up and speak out. However, even as we respond to these issues, I believe we are in danger of losing sight of what the main issue is. Maybe better stated, we are in danger of losing sight of *who* the main issue is.

What if the main issue is not poverty or sex trafficking, homosexuality or abortion? What if the main issue is *God*? More specifically, what if the main issue is the glory of God revealed in the gospel? And what might happen if we made *him* our focus instead? In a world marked by sexual immorality and sex slavery, the abandonment of children and the murder of children, racism and persecution, the needs of the poor and the neglect of the widow, how would we act if we fixed our gaze on the holiness, love, goodness, truth, justice, authority, and mercy of God revealed in the gospel?

These are the questions that compelled me to write my most recent book, *Counter*

Culture. This booklet focuses specifically on one of the issues covered in the book in order to help you begin thinking about this issue from a biblical perspective. As you do, my prayer is that your eyes might be opened to the needs of people in our culture and around the world and that you might be compelled by the call of Christ to engage this pressing social issue with compassion, conviction, and courage in the culture around you.

David Platt

REACHING THE UNREACHED

As we contemplate the massive physical needs in the world—needs we ought to address—if we are not careful, we run the risk of ignoring people's most pressing need. That need is not for water, food, family, freedom, safety, or equality. As urgent as all of these things are for men, women, and children around the world, they are surpassed in urgency by a much greater need.

That need—the most urgent need—is for the gospel.

THE MOST URGENT NEED

Jesus, of all people, knew the depth of people's physical needs. He had spent time with the sick, sat with the dying, and served the impoverished. When he saw the crowds, the Bible tells us "he had compassion for them," using words in the original language of the New Testament that portray a profound physical longing to provide for people with "every disease and every affliction" (Matthew 9:35-36). Yet his last words to his disciples show an even higher priority: in light of worldly suffering, over and above everything else, Jesus was calling them to speak.

You see, Jesus knew that as great as people's earthly needs were, their eternal need was far greater. When a paralytic was brought to him on a mat, Jesus said to him, "Son, your sins are forgiven" (Mark 2:5). He used this opportunity to teach a paralyzed man and the people around him that the ultimate priority of his coming was not to relieve suffering, as important and needed as that is. Instead, his ultimate priority in coming to the world was to sever the root of suffering: sin itself.

ETERNITY IN THE BALANCE

This is our—and everyone's—greatest need. Fundamentally, all people have sinned against God and are separated from him. Consequently, all of our lives not only on earth but also in eternity are at stake. Heaven and hell hang in the balance. God has made a way for all people to be reconciled to him through the life, death, and resurrection of Christ. All who receive him will experience eternal life, yet all who reject him suffer everlasting torment. This is the message of the gospel, and it is what people most need to hear.

Christ is not callous toward earthly needs.

But he is even more passionate about eternal needs. The reason he came was to reconcile people to God. He came not just to give the poor drinking water for their bodies but to give people living water for their souls. He came not just to give orphans and widows a family now but to give them a family forever. He came not just to free girls from slavery to sex but to free them (and those who abuse them) from slavery to sin. He came not just to make equality possible on earth but to make eternity possible in heaven.

DON'T MISS THE POINT

Because the gospel is the most pressing need in people's lives, the gospel informs the fundamental purpose of our lives. We who know the gospel have been given the greatest gift in all the world. We have good news of a glorious God who has come to deliver men, women, and children from all sin and all suffering for all time. Therefore, we cannot—we *must not*—stay silent with this gospel. Gospel possession requires gospel proclamation.

This is the major fallacy of social ministry in the church divorced from proclaiming the message of Christ. If all we do is meet people's physical needs while ignoring their spiritual need, we miss the entire point. Yet so often this is exactly what we settle for, and we do so because it's easier and less costly for us. It's far easier to give a cup of water to the thirsty and walk away than it is to give that same cup of water and stay around to share about the living water that comes through Christ alone. But yet again, as Christians we don't have the choice of disconnecting these two. We must proclaim the gospel as we provide for others' good. We are compelled to speak as we serve. We testify with our lips what we attest with our lives.

To be clear, giving a cup of water to the

poor is not contingent upon that person's confession of faith in Christ. Loving our neighbors as ourselves does not limit giving in this way. Instead, giving a cup of water to the poor is accompanied by sharing the good news of the gospel. True love for our neighbor requires nothing less. We care much about earthly suffering, but we care most about eternal suffering.[1]

Moreover, in God's good providence, it is in addressing eternal suffering that we are most effective in alleviating earthly suffering. After more than a decade of research on the effect of missionaries on the health of nations, sociologist Robert Woodberry came to the conclusion that "the work of missionaries . . . turns out to be the single largest factor in ensuring the health of nations."[2] Specifically, Woodberry contrasted the work of "conversionary Protestant" missionaries with "Protestant clergy financed by the state" and "Catholic missionaries prior to the 1960s." Woodberry observed, "Areas where Protestant missionaries had a significant presence in the past are on average more economically developed today, with comparatively better health, lower infant mortality, lower corruption, greater literacy, higher educational attainment (especially for women), and more robust membership in nongovernmental associations." In Woodberry's words, these conclusions landed on him like an "atomic bomb."[3]

THE CHURCH'S CENTRAL MISSION

But we are not surprised by Woodberry's findings when we consider what we see in Scripture. For the greatest way to achieve social and cultural transformation is not by focusing on social and cultural transformation, but by giving our lives to gospel proclamation—to telling others the good news of all God has done in Christ and calling them to follow him. The fruit of such salvation will be inevitable transformation—of lives, of families, of communities, and even of nations.

The central mission of the church in the world, then, is proclaiming the gospel to the world, and there is much work to be done, not only in our culture but among people around the world. Anthropological scholars have identified over eleven thousand different people groups in the world. Meanwhile, Jesus has called us to proclaim the gospel to all of them. "Make disciples of all nations," he says in the great commission, and the word for "nations" there is *ethne*, or ethnolinguistic groups. This commission is not just a general command to make disciples among as many people as possible. Instead, it is a specific command to make disciples among every people group in the world.

AN INTOLERABLE REALITY

You may wonder how we're doing in obeying Christ's command. Missiological scholars have attempted to identify how many of these eleven thousand people groups have been reached with the gospel. A people group is classified as "unreached" if less than 2 percent of the population is made up of Christians who confess the gospel and believe the Bible. In practical terms, for a people group to be "unreached" means that not only do individuals in that people group not believe the gospel, but because there is no church around them, no Christians among them, and in many cases no one attempting to get the gospel to them, most of them will die without even hearing it. So how many people groups are still unreached? More than six thousand—a population of at least two billion people.

When will the concept of unreached peoples become intolerable to the church?

What will it take to wake us up to the dearth of the gospel among the peoples of the world? What will it take to stir our hearts and lives for men and women whose souls are plunging into damnation without ever even hearing of salvation? This cannot be conceivable for people who confess the gospel. For if this gospel is true, and if our God is worthy of the praise of all people, then we must spend our lives and mobilize our churches for the spread of Christ's love to unreached people groups all around the world. Jesus has not given us a commission to consider; he has given us a command to obey.

Simply hearing about the number of unreached people groups and individuals can be overwhelming. Really, how can we make any difference? Gratefully, this is not a burden God intends for us to bear. He is the One who does the saving, and he is the One who sends out workers.

So how should we respond? We must begin by hearing what God's Word has to say about this great need.

WHAT DOES GOD'S WORD SAY ABOUT THE UNREACHED?

Read through the following questions and the corresponding Scriptures. Take time to think about and meditate on these truths.

How do those who have no access to the gospel stand before God?

"The wrath of God is revealed from heaven against all ungodliness and unrighteousness of men, who by their unrighteousness suppress the truth. For what can be known about God is plain to them, because God has shown it to them. For his invisible attributes, namely, his eternal power and divine nature, have been clearly perceived, ever since the creation of

the world, in the things that have been made. So they are without excuse." ROMANS 1:18-20

"You were dead in the trespasses and sins in which you once walked, following the course of this world, following the prince of the power of the air, the spirit that is now at work in the sons of disobedience—among whom we all once lived in the passions of our flesh, carrying out the desires of the body and the mind, and were by nature children of wrath, like the rest of mankind." EPHESIANS 2:1-3

"I was brought forth in iniquity, and in sin did my mother conceive me." PSALM 51:5

"All have sinned and fall short of the glory of God." ROMANS 3:23

As descendants of Adam, all people are born with a sinful nature and stand guilty before God. This means that those who have not yet heard the gospel are not innocent. Scripture teaches that everyone suppresses the truth of God that is known from creation, preferring idols over the worship of the one true God. Unreached people groups need the grace of God in the gospel because they are guilty of rebellion.

How does Scripture speak about hell and the judgment of God?

"An hour is coming when all who are in the tombs will hear his voice and come out, those who have done good to the resurrection of life, and those who have done evil to the resurrection of judgment." JOHN 5:28-29

"When the Lord Jesus is revealed from heaven with his mighty angels in flaming fire, inflicting vengeance on those who do not know God and on those who do not obey the gospel of our Lord Jesus. They will suffer the

punishment of eternal destruction, away from the presence of the Lord and from the glory of his might." 2 THESSALONIANS 1:7-9

"He will render to each one according to his works: to those who by patience in well-doing seek for glory and honor and immortality, he will give eternal life; but for those who are self-seeking and do not obey the truth, but obey unrighteousness, there will be wrath and fury. There will be tribulation and distress for every human being who does evil, the Jew first and also the Greek, but glory and honor and peace for everyone who does good, the Jew first and also the Greek. For God shows no partiality." ROMANS 2:6-11

"[The one who worships the beast] will drink the wine of God's wrath, poured full strength into the cup of his anger, and he will be tormented with fire and sulfur in the presence of the holy angels and in the presence of the

Lamb. And the smoke of their torment goes up forever and ever, and they have no rest, day or night, these worshipers of the beast and its image, and whoever receives the mark of its name." REVELATION 14:10-11

"I saw a great white throne and him who was seated on it. From his presence earth and sky fled away, and no place was found for them. And I saw the dead, great and small, standing before the throne, and books were opened. Then another book was opened, which is the book of life. And the dead were judged by what was written in the books, according to what they had done. And the sea gave up the dead who were in it, Death and Hades gave up the dead who were in them, and they were judged, each one of them, according to what they had done. Then Death and Hades were thrown into the lake of fire. This is the second death, the lake of fire. And if anyone's name was not found

written in the book of life, he was thrown into the lake of fire. REVELATION 20:11-15

Some of the most sobering passages in all of Scripture are those that describe hell. God's judgment is a fearful reality: all those who have not repented of their sin and trusted in Christ will spend eternity separated from him in conscious torment. This is the just punishment for sinning against an infinitely holy God, and it applies to everyone outside of Christ—unreached people groups as well as those who have heard and rejected the gospel.

What is the church's mission? Does it include all people groups?

"Jesus came and said to them, 'All authority in heaven and on earth has been given to me. Go therefore and make disciples of all nations, baptizing them in the name of the Father and of the Son and of the Holy Spirit, teaching

them to observe all that I have commanded you. And behold, I am with you always, to the end of the age.'" MATTHEW 28:18-20

"[Jesus] opened [his disciples'] minds to understand the Scriptures, and said to them, 'Thus it is written, that the Christ should suffer and on the third day rise from the dead, and that repentance and forgiveness of sins should be proclaimed in his name to all nations, beginning from Jerusalem. You are witnesses of these things.'" LUKE 24:45-48

"You [apostles] will receive power when the Holy Spirit has come upon you, and you will be my [Jesus'] witnesses in Jerusalem and in all Judea and Samaria, and to the end of the earth." ACTS 1:8

"I make it my ambition to preach the gospel, not where Christ has already been named, lest I build on someone else's foundation, but as it

is written, 'Those who have never been told of him will see, and those who have never heard will understand.'" ROMANS 15:20-21

"After this I looked, and behold, a great multitude that no one could number, from every nation, from all tribes and peoples and languages, standing before the throne and before the Lamb, clothed in white robes, with palm branches in their hands, and crying out with a loud voice, 'Salvation belongs to our God who sits on the throne, and to the Lamb!'"
REVELATION 7:9-10

Christ's command is clear: we are to make disciples of *"all* nations" (Matthew 28:19, emphasis added). We do not have the option—nor should we wish for it—of withholding the good news of the gospel from any people group. One day all tribes, peoples, and languages will be standing around the throne, giving praise to the Lamb who has purchased them with his blood.

Must people explicitly believe the gospel in order to be saved?

"How then will they call on him in whom they have not believed? And how are they to believe in him of whom they have never heard? And how are they to hear without someone preaching? And how are they to preach unless they are sent? As it is written, 'How beautiful are the feet of those who preach the good news!' But they have not all obeyed the gospel. For Isaiah says, 'Lord, who has believed what he has heard from us?' So faith comes from hearing, and hearing through the word of Christ." ROMANS 10:14-17

"There is salvation in no one else, for there is no other name under heaven given among men by which we must be saved." ACTS 4:12

"Jesus said to him, 'I am the way, and the truth, and the life. No one comes to the Father except through me.'" JOHN 14:6

An individual must place his or her faith in Jesus Christ (as he is presented in the gospel) in order to be saved. A general knowledge of God apart from the truth of Christ's life, death, and resurrection is not sufficient. This is why we must explicitly communicate the truths of the gospel to those who have never heard. They must repent and believe in Jesus in order to be forgiven of their sins and have eternal life.

A CALL TO COUNTER CULTURE

Christ's call in our lives is not to comfort in our culture. Christ in us actually compels us to counter our culture. Not to quietly sit and watch evolving cultural trends, and not to subtly shift our views amid changing cultural tides, but to courageously share and show our convictions through what we say and how we live, even (or especially) when these convictions contradict the popular positions of our day. And to do all of this not with conceited minds or calloused hearts, but with the humble compassion of Christ on constant display in everything we say and do.

Isn't this, after all, the essence of what it means to follow Christ? "If anyone would come after me, let him deny himself and take up his cross daily and follow me" (Luke 9:23). Talk about countercultural! In a world where everything revolves around yourself—protect yourself, promote yourself, comfort yourself, take care of yourself—Jesus says, "Crucify yourself. Put aside all self-preservation in order to live for God's glorification, no matter what that means for you in the culture around you."

Isn't this the main issue in any culture? Isn't *he* the main issue in any culture? And what might happen if we made *God* our focus? In a world marked by sex slavery and sexual immorality, the abandonment of children and the murder of children, racism and persecution, the needs of the poor and the neglect of the widow, how would we act if we fixed our gaze on the holiness, love, goodness, truth, justice, authority, and mercy of God revealed in the gospel?

The gospel is the lifeblood of Christianity, and it provides the foundation for countering culture. For when we truly believe the gospel, we begin to realize that the gospel not only *compels* Christians to confront social issues in the culture around us. The gospel actually *creates* confrontation with the culture around—and within—us.

The Eternal Offense

The idea that God became a man—Jesus—is outlandish to multitudes around the world.

More than a billion Muslims believe that God would never debase himself by becoming a man. Hundreds of millions of others think it preposterous that a man could be divine.

But the gospel's offense goes further than simply claiming that God became a man. The gospel asserts that not only has God become a man but this God-man has been crucified. This is foolishness to contemporary men and women. Imagine taking a successful, well-dressed American man with a nice job, big house, and cool car and a freethinking American woman who thrives on her independence and leading them to a garbage dump, where a naked man hangs by nails on a tree, covered in blood, and telling them, "This is your God." They will laugh at you, may possibly feel sorry for the man, and almost certainly will move on with their lives.

Yet the offense of the gospel reaches its peak when you tell them that their eternal destiny is dependent on whether they believe the man hanging there is their God—the Lord, Judge, Savior, and King of all creation. As soon as you say, "If you follow him, you will experience eternal life; if not, you will experience everlasting hell," you will find yourself across a line of utmost contention in contemporary culture (and in the contemporary church, for that matter).

The gospel claims that eternity is at stake in how you and I respond to Jesus.

The Fundamental Question

According to the Bible, heaven is a glorious reality for those who trust in Jesus. It is a place of full reconciliation and complete restoration where sin, suffering, pain, and sorrow will finally cease, and men and women who have trusted in Christ will live in perfect harmony with God and each other forever and ever.

The Bible also teaches that hell is a dreadful reality for those who turn from Jesus. It's a reality about which Jesus spoke much. Tim Keller observes, "If Jesus, the Lord of Love and Author of Grace spoke about hell more often, and in a more vivid, blood-curdling manner than anyone else, it must be a crucial truth."[4] This "crucial truth" flows directly from all we've discovered to this point.

Every man and woman has turned from God to self, and if nothing changes before they die, hell will be the God-given punishment for this sinful, self-exalting choice. Those who rebel against God on earth will receive the just penalty for the path they have chosen. Now of course no one, no matter how evil, would choose hell knowing the horror it entails. Scripture describes hell as a place where people will weep and gnash their teeth in a smoke of torment that rises without rest for all who reside there (see Matthew 8:12;

Revelation 14:11). No one knowingly wills to experience this. Yet by ultimately willing against God on earth, sinners' de facto destination is damnation in eternity.

When you put all these truths in the gospel together, you realize that the most offensive and countercultural claim in Christianity is not what Christians believe about homosexuality or abortion, marriage or religious liberty. Instead, the most offensive claim in Christianity is that God is the Creator, Owner, and Judge of every person on the planet. Every one of us stands before him guilty of sin, and the only way to be reconciled to him is through faith in Jesus, the crucified Savior and risen King. All who trust in his love will experience everlasting life while all who turn from his lordship will suffer everlasting death.

So we arrive at the fundamental question: Do you believe the gospel?

Conviction

If we truly believe the truths of the gospel, then we must act in addressing social issues. I want to call Christians to conviction. We live in a unique time in Western culture, when the moral landscape is rapidly changing. As a result, we have many opportunities to stand upon and speak about divine truth. May we not let this moment pass. Elizabeth Rundle Charles, commenting on Martin Luther's confrontation of key issues in his day, says:

> It is the truth which is assailed in any age which tests our fidelity. . . . If I profess with the loudest voice and clearest exposition every portion of the truth of God except precisely that point which the world and the devil are at that moment attacking, I am not confessing Christ, however boldly I

may be professing Christianity. Where the battle rages, there the loyalty of the soldier is proven, and to be steady on all the battle fronts besides is mere flight and disgrace if he flinches at that point.[5]

Indeed, battles are raging over a number of social issues in our culture today. Just decades ago, Francis Schaeffer wrote:

We as Bible-believing evangelical Christians are locked in a battle. This is not a friendly gentleman's discussion. It is a life and death conflict between the spiritual hosts of wickedness and those who claim the name of Christ. . . . But do we really believe that we are in a life and death battle? . . . Where is the clear voice speaking to the crucial issues of the day with distinctively

biblical, Christian answers? With tears
we must say it is not there and that a
large segment of the evangelical world
has become seduced by the world spirit
of this present age. And more than this,
we can expect the future to be a further
disaster if the evangelical world does
not take a stand for biblical truth and
morality in the full spectrum of life.[6]

May this not be said of our generation.
May we not sin through silence. May we realize that not to speak is to speak. Ultimately,
may it be said of us that we not only held
firm to the gospel, but that we spoke clearly
with the gospel to the most pressing issues
of our day.

Compassion

In addition to calling us to conviction, I
want to call us to compassion. Matthew 9

tells us that "when [Jesus] saw the crowds, he had compassion for them, because they were harassed and helpless, like sheep without a shepherd" (verse 36). One of my hopes is that God would give us grace to see what he sees. To see the poor, the hungry, and the neglected as he sees them. To perceive those crushed by political, economic, or ethnic oppression from his perspective. To care for the baby in the womb as well as the baby's mother as God cares for them. To love the orphan and the widow, the homosexual and the heterosexual, the immigrant and the immoral as God loves them.

Based upon his love, I want to call us to action. "You shall love your neighbor as yourself," Jesus commands (Matthew 22:39). John writes, "Let us not love in word or talk but in deed and in truth" (1 John 3:18). The last thing I want to do is to divorce biblical, theological, and ethical principles from individual, family, and church practice. The goal of this booklet (and my larger book *Counter Culture*) is not information about the gospel and social issues; it is application of the gospel to social issues. I want to explore the unreached and other issues not with a self-righteous complacency that makes us content to wring our hands in pious concern, but with a self-sacrificing commitment to be whoever God calls us to be, go wherever God tells us to go, give whatever God compels us to give, and serve whomever God leads us to serve.

Inevitably, God will lead us to act in different ways. Not every one of us can give equal attention to every issue. Nor *should* any one of us do so, for God sovereignly puts us in unique positions and places with unique privileges and opportunities to influence the culture around us. But what is necessary for all of us is to view cultural issues through the lens of biblical truth and to speak such truth with conviction whenever we have the chance. Then, based on consistent conviction, we seek how individually as Christians and collectively in our churches the Spirit of Christ is leading us to compassionate action in our culture.

In order to help us in this, I've included some initial suggestions for practical requests you and I can pray, potential ways you or I might participate in cultural engagement with the gospel, and biblical truths we must proclaim regarding the unreached. These suggestions will also direct you to a website where you can explore more specific steps that you might take. I encourage you to consider all these suggestions and to humbly, boldly, seriously, and prayerfully consider what God is directing you to do. Let's not merely contemplate the Word of God in the world around us; let's do what it says (see James 1:22-25).

Courage

Acting with conviction and compassion will require courage, to be sure. It is increasingly countercultural to stand upon unshakable truth in this ever-shifting time. The cost of biblical conviction in contemporary culture is growing steeper every day, and we are not far removed from sharing more soberly in the sufferings of Christ. Doubtless this is why more and more "Christians" today are stepping away from gospel truth. Fear is a powerful force, leading more and more "churches" today to accommodation and adaptation instead of confrontation with the surrounding culture. Consequently, I believe Schaeffer's words are appropriate:

> We need a young generation and others
> who will be willing to stand in loving
> confrontation, but real confrontation,
> in contrast to the mentality of constant

accommodation with the current forms of the world spirit as they surround us today, and in contrast to the way in which so much of *evangelicalism* has developed the automatic mentality to accommodate at each successive point.[7]

My hope is that we would heed this challenge. For it is not ultimately a challenge from Schaeffer; it is a challenge from Christ. He says to us:

"Do not fear those who kill the body but cannot kill the soul. Rather fear him who can destroy both soul and body in hell. . . . Everyone who acknowledges me before men, I also will acknowledge before my Father who is in heaven, but whoever denies me before men, I also will deny before my Father who is in heaven. . . . Whoever finds his life will lose it, and

whoever loses his life for my sake will find it." MATTHEW 10:28, 32-33, 39

The gospel of Christ is not a call to cultural compromise in the face of fear. Instead, the gospel of Christ is a call to counter-cultural crucifixion—death to self in the face of earthly opposition for the sake of eternal reward.

My hope is that we would believe the gospel of Christ and that our belief would move us to engage our culture. My prayer is that God will open our eyes to the needs of people in our culture and around the world, bring us to our knees in tears and prayers on their behalf, and cause us to rise with conviction, compassion, and courage to humbly spread the truth of God while selflessly showing the love of God, all in hopeful anticipation of the day when sin, suffering, immorality, and injustice will finally be no more.

WHAT CAN I DO ABOUT THE UNREACHED?

Below you'll see suggestions for how we might respond to those who still need to hear the gospel.

Pray

Use the following prayer guide to help you intercede on behalf of the unreached:

- Ask God to open your heart to the plight of unreached people groups around the world.
- Ask God to awaken many churches and individual Christians to the urgent spiritual need that exists among the unreached.
- Pray that God would send out gospel workers to labor among the unreached.
- Pray that God would open doors for gospel proclamation among people

groups that have been resistant to missionaries.

- Ask God what your role should be in taking the gospel to an unreached people group—would he have *you* go?
- Ask God to provide resources for you and your church so that you might give sacrificially to missionaries who work among the unreached.

Participate

Use the following suggestions to think through how you can engage unreached people groups with the gospel:

- Begin praying for specific unreached people groups with other members of your church (in small group, Bible study, Sunday school, etc.).
- Give sacrificially through your local church as it sends and supports missionaries. Consider what luxuries

you might forgo to increase your
support.

- Visit websites like peoplegroups.org,
  joshuaproject.net, and operationworld
  .org to learn more about the unreached
  and how you can engage them.
- Write letters of encouragement to
  missionaries that your church supports.
- Speak with your church about the
  possibility of taking a short-term
  mission trip and be open to how the
  Lord might use this experience in your
  future for the sake of the unreached.
- Find out whether there are members
  of an unreached people group in your
  own community (exchange students,
  immigrants, refugees, etc.) so that you
  can befriend them and engage them
  with the gospel.
- Make disciples in your own community
  as you pray about how the Lord might

use your gifts and abilities across the globe.

Proclaim

Consider the following biblical foundations to direct your thoughts and actions toward the unreached:

- Matthew 28:19: "Go . . . and make disciples of all nations."
- Romans 10:14-15: "How then will they call on him in whom they have not believed? And how are they to believe in him of whom they have never heard? And how are they to hear without someone preaching? And how are they to preach unless they are sent?"
- Matthew 9:37-38: "[Jesus] said to his disciples, 'The harvest is plentiful, but the laborers are few; therefore pray earnestly to the Lord of the harvest to send out laborers into his harvest.'"

For additional information and resources to help you engage this issue in the culture around you, visit CounterCultureBook.com /Unreached.

LET US NOT STAY SILENT

Let's not stay silent with the gospel. Let's not allow fear in our culture to muzzle our faith in Christ. And let's not enable indecision to rule our lives. Let's not permit delay to characterize our days. We don't have to ask what the will of God is in the world; he has made it clear. He wants his people to provide for the poor, to value the unborn, to care for orphans and widows, to rescue people from slavery, to defend marriage, to war against sexual immorality in all its forms in every area of our lives, to love our neighbors as ourselves regardless of their ethnicity, to proclaim and practice truth regardless of the risk, and to proclaim the gospel to all nations. Of these things we are sure.

So pray to God, participate with God, and proclaim the gospel. And do these things not because you have a low-grade sense of guilt that you ought to act, but do them because you have a high-grade sense of grace that makes you want to act. Do them because you know that you were once impoverished in your sin, a slave to Satan, orphaned from God, and alone in this world. Yet God reached down his mercy-filled hand into your sin-soaked heart and through the sacrifice of his only begotten Son on a blood-stained cross, he lifted you up to new life by his alluring love. You now have nothing to fear and nothing to lose because you are robed in the riches of Christ and safe in the security of Christ.

And pray to God, participate with God, and proclaim the gospel not under a utopian illusion that you or I or anyone or everyone together can rid this world of pain and suffering. That responsibility belongs to the resurrected Christ, and he will do it when he returns. But until that day, do with an undivided heart whatever he calls you to do. Some will say that these problems are complex, and one person, family, or church can't really make much of a difference. In many respects, this is true, and each of these issues is extremely complicated. But don't underestimate what God will do in and through one person, one family, or one church for the spread of his gospel and the sake of his glory in our culture. So do these things with the unshakable conviction that God has put you in this culture at this time for a reason. He has called you to himself, he has saved you by his Son, he has filled you with his Spirit, he has captured you with his love, and he is compelling you by his Word to counter our culture by proclaiming his Kingdom, not worried about what it will cost you because you are confident that God himself is your great reward.

NOTES

1. John Piper's address at the Lausanne Conference on World Evangelization in 2010 was a challenge to minister to both earthly and eternal needs. See John Piper, "Making Known the Manifold Wisdom of God through Prison and Prayer," Desiring God, October 19, 2010, www.desiringgod.org/conference -messages/making-known-the-manifold-wisdom-of -god-through-prison-and-prayer.
2. Andrea Palpant Dilley, "The Surprising Discovery about Those Colonialist, Proselytizing Missionaries," *Christianity Today* 58, no. 1 (January/February 2014): 36.
3. Ibid., 38–40.
4. Tim Keller, "The Importance of Hell," Redeemer Presbyterian Church, August 2009, www.redeemer .com/redeemer-report/article/the_importance_of_hell.
5. Elizabeth Rundle Charles, *Chronicles of the Schönberg-Cotta Family* (New York: M. W. Dodd, 1864), 321.
6. Francis Schaeffer, *A Christian View of the Church*, volume 4 in The Complete Works of Francis Schaeffer: A Christian Worldview (Wheaton, IL: Crossway, 1982), 316–317, 401.
7. Ibid, 410.

ARE *YOU* READY TO
COUNTER CULTURE?

Everywhere we turn, battle lines are being drawn. Seemingly overnight, culture has shifted to the point where right and wrong are no longer measured by universal truth but by popular opinion.

In *Counter Culture*, David Platt shows Christians how to actively take a stand on such issues as poverty, sex trafficking, marriage, abortion, racism, and religious liberty and challenges us to become passionate, unwavering voices for Christ.

Additional study materials are available online and in a bookstore near you. To learn more about how you can counter culture, please visit us at www.counterculturebook.com.